to my little b
I love you
much! xoxo
jen jen

Lavender Blood
Madeline Rose & Jennifer Rose

BAMBAZ Press
Los Angeles. 2017

Cover Art: Baz Here
Book Design: Baz Here
Editor: Bambi Here
Photos: Madeline Rose

ISBN13: 9781545406571

BAMBAZ Press
548 S Spring Street
Suite 1201
Los Angeles, CA 90013

contact: bambi@bambazpress.com

Dedicated to Bubbie and Papa
(Mom and Dad)
Forever in our hearts

Where you lead, I will follow
Anywhere that you tell me to
If you need, you need me to be with you
I will follow where you lead.

–Carole King

TABLE OF CONTENTS

MADELINE ROSE

JENNIFER ROSE

MADELINE ROSE

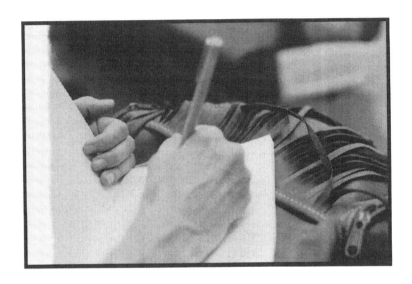

WRITING

writing is
the escape from pain
the cure to pain
the door to pain

UNIVERSE

we are like the sun, the moon and the stars
our love will always be there like the stars
but only a couple times a year will we meet
like a solar eclipse
we will cross paths for only a while
but this universe is far too large for us
meteors will strike us and interrupt our silence
but shooting stars shall fly across the sky
and we shall wish upon them
as if there was one every second
and we wish
we wish
that there could be a solar eclipse
that lasted for all of eternity
but things that like that are only temporary

PLUVIOPHILE

she was a fragile girl
fogged glass and
hand-drawn smiles
she was a broken girl
fragmented radios and
scratched vinyls
she was a sad girl
spilt coffee and
unfinished books
she was the rain
itself and the beauty
of it was that no
matter how loud the
storm was, someone
for sure loved her

YOUR DUMB RECOLLECTION

who knew a tiny person
could hold all the memories
but her dumb recollection
kept nothing at all
that peanut brain
can't hold a damn thing

INFATUATION

enjoy the silence
like that could ever happen
I want someone to love me
but how can someone love me
if I can't even love myself?

STARVING

I starve to feel something
craving for absolutely anything
just to feel full
just to feel normal
I am craving for anything
anything at all
and the one thing I want
to make me feel full
is something out of reach
so for now I crave nothing
the feeling of absolutely nothing is the worst
but at least it gives me something to feel

SCARS

I look at my wrist
the scars are fading
they are battle scars
but show great weakness
each scar represents a lost battle
I gave in and let those scars happen
it shows weakness and that I gave in
I let this happen
they are fading
but will always be there
'cause they are scars
maybe not on my skin
but in my mind

UNSPOKEN

we didn't have to say it
this was a goodbye kiss
a kiss which drowned
in 'I love you'

BLURB 15

I wish it was easy to be happy like it is to be sad

FORGETFUL FLOWERS

I have these flowers
wilting
soon to be nothing
becoming one with the soil
they lay in a place where I can see them
dying a little each day
they are in a sunny place
but no one waters it
this reminds me of everything around me
including myself
there is a little pink bud that is closing
dying

one day I will be those flowers
I will die and the flowers will soon
fall into their own demise
each wilted flower
will represent a memory of me
I will be forgotten when I am gone
I soon will disappear from everything
I will be one with the soil
banished from existence

EVERYDAY

everyday for years my eyes tend
to have purple bags
under them from lack of sleep
my cheeks flushed
eyes glossed over in threatening tears
until I'm all cried out
until I saw you
until my heart turned lavender
I didn't cry because I was sad
I was crying because you are beautiful
and I'm so goddamn happy

HERE

my heartbeat is in my throat and I can't breathe
is this what it feels like?
so painful yet so painless
warm fuzzy all wrapping around me
but I grew cold and no one was holding me
and then I felt nothing
then I felt a wave of everything

ETERNITY

I didn't think I loved sleeping as much once you
entered my dreams, it felt real
I know I shouldn't wish to sleep forever but if my
dreams are like this with you...
I would never want to see the light of day
ever again

ENVY

I envy his ability to be ecstatic about the tiniest
things
I envy his love for the world no matter if it is shit
I envy how he appreciates each breath he takes
I envy the way he refuses to let himself fall out
of love
—without ever finding the meaning
I envy him for everything he is

LOVE THINGS

I smiled at you, but all you saw was her
and I'm scared I'll never be her

I kissed the person I liked goodbye and now I feel
like I can fly

you know how when you lay in bed
after a day at the beach or at a theme park,
you feel like you are in a wave or on a ride?
that's how it felt when I laid down
and felt your lips on mine.
I can't get the feeling out of my head
how am I supposed to sleep now?

you're my favorite thing
you're my favorite sight
you're my favorite sound
you're my favorite feeling
you're my favorite everything

today I was sad
you looked at me and smiled
but smiling hurt me
so I didn't back
later you looked at me
and smiled
I barely smiled back but it still hurt
moments later you looked back again
and you smiled, laughing
lips curling up, eyes almost shut
god, you were just too beautiful
to not smile back at

today I was sad
but you made me so happy
if only you knew you had that impact on me

BUTTERFLIES

it isn't the butterflies that scare me,
it is the fact that I can't wipe that dumb smile
off my face when I see you

AND WE DANCED

and we danced
my head against his chest
his heart beating quickly
my hand intertwined with his bigger one
his opposite delicate hand on my waist
as we sway back and forth
and even in a room full of people
all I saw was him

PAPA

standing tall
you have your heavy leather jacket on
in 100° weather
only to have three more layers under
consisting of a flannel,
an undershirt, and a tank top
I don't know how you survived
this ridiculous California weather
but you pulled it off...
oh and you had heavy corduroy jeans
on with your New Balance shoes
you had dog treats in your right pocket
and in the left melted candies
you saved for my brother and me
you would drive us home
in your year 2000 Lexus RX 350
that smelled of you
I miss you and everything reminds me of you
you liked chickens and whenever someone
is eating chicken tenders I think of you

I'LL BE SEEING YOU

you left me three days after my birthday
and I still believe you waited for my birthday
to pass
and I can't thank you enough for every moment
I got to spend with you
sometimes I think I should've done this or that
but I'm glad I even knew you
you are the best thing that happened to me,
but left too early
I'll think of you when I graduate high school,
walk down the aisle, have my first kid,
and every waking moment I spend till my demise,
but don't worry
I'll be seeing you

LOST

I want to get lost in New York
it's not everyone's ideal but it is what I want
the comfort of a busy, lovable place is soothing
there's not one specific person you can't aspire
to be
I want to get lost in New York
smell the familiar scent of car exhaust
let it flow through me and remind me where I am
hear the constant taxis trying to get by
let them honk and remind me where I am
see the diverse groups of people
let them be different and remind me where I am
taste warm, crunchy churros bought from a tiny cart
off 3rd Street
let it be the best thing I've ever tasted
and remind me where I am
touch the dirty railings to get down to the subways
let me remember the billions of people
who have been remind where I am
I want to get lost in New York

LAVENDER BLOOD

and the only thing that could fog my mind
was the lavender blood he swam in

JENNIFER ROSE

SHELLS

I was wearing a white eyelet dress
daisies
limited to brief moments of happiness
it's not for everybody
poetry
dissatisfaction
distraction
running wild
small pink shells
someday I will take them out again
but for now they will sit on the shelf
praying to be loved

WANDER*LUST*

Santiago
Sao Paulo
Serbia
Spain
some of the S's that I loved

lovers so wrong
they all felt right

Americans bored me
in my 20's
in my 30's
in my 40's

whispers in my ear
with a foreign tongue
even take out the trash
sounds sexy

CHANDELIER

I danced with him
under the chandelier
swaying
candles burning
he called me Bubbles
in his big love
take all of my poems
it will be our secret

BURSTING

I am bursting like a firework
inside a pink bubble
that floats
rising from the milky bathwater
hovering like an angel
on the side of the antique bathtub
I sit
soaking away your memory
every bubble that pops
sets free the fierce love
that my heart swims in
I am reborn
knowing
that letting you go
is the only way
I will find myself again

ILLUSIONS OF GRANDEUR

when the world was in color
and we were young
we sold root beer floats
with Häagen-Dazs ice cream
in Beverly Hills

you know the rest
the blue plastic mugs
handle and all

years later
my mom told me
we lost money on every sale
five-dollars worth for 50 cents a pop
illusions of grandeur
under the hot sun
in another world

SILVER LINING

you were my silver lining
brightened up my darkest day
when depression came to visit
you scared it far away
you promised me I had your love
and you would never leave

I pray you stay away from me
and let my heart to grieve

45

he left wanting more
which is the only way
I ever want him to leave

BLOOD

let me cut my finger
watch it bleed this paper red
the vision of platelets smearing words
down the page revealing
the depths of my scarred heart

he said goodbye to my children today
what is the only thing worse
than having your heart broken?
watching him break theirs

DESCENT

you were an angel
in my life
how foolish I was
spending my time
with you,
trying to describe
hell to you,
rather than living
in your light

TURN UP THE MUSIC

alone in my head
I hear the screams
—shrieks so loud
I cover my ears but that only makes
the sound louder
the pain worse
coming from inside my head
screams so loud dogs around me howl
spirits stir
only they can hear my pain
my silent noise
maybe
one day
the screams will stop
but until then
I will turn up the music

ROADBLOCK

I hate him for leaving
for breaking his vow
he did it before
I was foolish
to think this time
would be different
he was afraid of abandonment
so was I
we tiptoed over commitment
understanding one's pain is insight
but it doesn't take the roadblock down

GUTTED

no drink or pill
to smooth the edges
of his jagged knife

he carved J & S
gutted the redwood
broke open bark
beheading the grass

1,095 days
molecules to vapor

MUTILATED HEART

deprivation
collapse
annihilation
massacre
slaughter
execution
assassination
eradication
void

your absence—
the language of my mutilated heart

BULLETPROOF

his calculated indecision
his certain ambiguity
his clarity of confusion

downing his third cup of coffee on Larchmont
he said,
"our love is addictive, radioactive"

"that's the problem with recovery,
too many slogans," I said

don't believe everything you think

I NEED TO LOVE YOU

I need to love you
one more time—
just one more time
I need to forget you
one last time—
one very last time
I need to choke you
and wake you up
because while you're finding yourself—
you are losing me

LOVE INTOLERANT

unreachable
untouchable
unrecognizable

from here
to gone

split
splat
poof

one day
I will
make sense
of his goodbye

CARVINGS AND POEMS

daily patterns of lines and roads
one destination

shade of a broken soul
tired of carvings and poems

forever remaining my beginning
even though it is the hungry end

BLINK

I forget during moments of holding hands, dancing together to Mama Mia, fits of giggles, tummies aching from years of laughter which seem to permeate between us so naturally.

I forget time is creeping near us and trying to put its heinous hands on her and slowly steal her from me.

When did she get taller than me,
stronger than me,
wiser than me?

I thought she was all mine.
Ivory skin and jet black hair from birth.

I dreamt her when I was sixteen.
A dark tousled-haired bubbly little girl.
I even dreamt her freckles.
Filling my heart and the vacuous hole that I had which haunted my womb until she occupied it, emerging from my insides, into my arms.

How will I ever survive her leaving me?
I thought foolishly it would last forever.

Making her lunches, combing out her endless tangles, praising her for sleeping in her own bed, terrified now of her never asking to sleep in mine again.

I yearn for the days of strangers stopping me on the street, mid-stroll, diaper bag in hand trying to hold

my vanilla latte in one hand and her pacifier in the other at the same time. Strangers with foreign words falling from their mouths...
"It flies by you know, mine is in college, don't blink!"

College? College and these delusional women were so far removed from our daily routine of 2 p.m. nap, 5 p.m. bath and 7 p.m. first taste of creamed sweet potatoes from the clear glass jar with the word organic splashed across the front.

College? Were they insane? She had yet to hand me my first Mother's Day card she made me her first year in preschool after my own mother died. It was a pink handprint on red construction paper that read, "I love you Mommy."
It made losing my mother molecularly less painful because I was reminded I am her mother.

My baby girl, my fierce Snow White fluttering around like a butterfly. Happy, joyous and free.

College was too far away to even glimpse. Mommy and Maddie. Maddie and Mommy. Me and her, her and me. I didn't know where she ended and I began. The dynamic duo that now share jeans, mascara and cycles.

Now I have become the stranger on the street who stops young mothers mid-stroll, warning them not to blink, urging them to enjoy the sleepless nights and endless diapers, trying in vain to protect them of the fatal mistake I made.
I blinked.

Jennifer Rose is a writer – always has been since she was in the third grade. Her journals were covered with poems, musings, and humor. No wonder—her father was Mickey Rose—a film and television writer. She is also the sister of Quincy Rose, writer and filmmaker. Jennifer is a member of the Los Angeles Poets & Writers Collective and is published in *I Went to Ralph's to Get a Chicken* and *I'll Have Wednesday, Volume 3* and *Volume 4*. She lives in Los Angeles with her two children (and three cats). Jennifer is busy working on a documentary about her dad and her forthcoming book. Any night, you might find her singing and dancing around her living room.

Madeline Rose has been writing poetry and short stories since she was eight years old. She loved sharing her writing with her Papa—Mickey Rose, a film and television writer. Her passions include singing, dancing (especially musicals) and dark room photography. Madeline has been published in *I'll Have Wednesday, Volume 4*. She is attending high school in Los Angeles and is currently working on her next solo book of poetry. Madeline loves playing the ukulele, New York City, and sloths.

Made in the USA
Middletown, DE
13 July 2017